Community Helpers

Lifeguards

by Sandra J. Christian, M.Ed.

Consultant:
Mike McKenna
Advisor, Florida Beach Patrol Chiefs Association
Chairman for Public Education
United States Lifesaving Association

Bridgestone Books
an imprint of Capstone Press
Mankato, Minnesota

Bridgestone Books are published by Capstone Press
151 Good Counsel Drive, P.O. Box 669, Mankato, Minnesota 56002
http://www.capstone-press.com

Library of Congress Cataloging-in-Publication Data
Christian, Sandra J.
  Lifeguards/by Sandra J. Christian.
  p. cm.—(Community helpers)
  Includes bibliographical references (p.24) and index.
  Summary: A simple introduction to the work lifeguards do, discussing where they
work, what tools they use, and how they are important to the communities they serve.
  ISBN 0-7368-1129-X
  1. Lifeguards—Juvenile literature. [1. Lifeguards. 2. Occupations.] I. Title.
II. Community helpers (Mankato, Minn.)
GV838.72 .C75 2002
797.2'1'0289—dc21   2001003329

Editorial Credits

Megan Schoeneberger, editor; Karen Risch, product planning editor; Linda Clavel, cover
    production designer; Katy Kudela, photo researcher

Photo Credits

Capstone Press/Gary Sundermeyer, cover, 4, 6, 14, 18; Gregg Andersen, 16
Daniel E. Hodges, 20
Index Stock Imagery/Larry Lawfer, 12
Photri-Microstock, 8
Shaffer Photography/James L. Shaffer, 10

1 2 3 4 5 6 07 06 05 04 03 02

Table of Contents

Lifeguards

Lifeguards watch people in and around water. They make sure people swim and play safely. Lifeguards help swimmers in emergencies. An emergency is a sudden danger. Someone drowning is a type of emergency.

What Lifeguards Do

Lifeguards do many jobs. They watch people swim. They help people who are hurt or drowning. They make sure people wait in line at the diving board. They tell swimmers at pools not to run. They warn swimmers at beaches about dangerous rip currents.

rip current
a channel of water flowing away from shore

Where Lifeguards Work

Lifeguards work at many swimming places. They watch swimmers at pools and lakes. They work at ocean or river beaches. Lifeguards work at hotels, water parks, and recreation centers. They work outdoors and indoors.

water park
a swimming place that has
slides and other play areas

Types of Lifeguards

Many lifeguards watch swimmers at swimming pools. Waterfront lifeguards watch swimmers at lakes and rivers. Surf lifeguards protect swimmers at ocean beaches. Head lifeguards are in charge of other lifeguards.

What Lifeguards Wear

Lifeguards wear clothing that can get wet. They wear swimsuits. They might wear t-shirts or jackets that say they are lifeguards. Outdoor lifeguards wear hats or sunglasses. They use sunscreen that will not wash off in water. Sunscreen protects their skin from the sun.

Tools Lifeguards Use

Lifeguards use many tools. They blow whistles to warn swimmers who break the rules. They use rescue tubes or rescue boards to help swimmers float. Lifeguards might use boats to reach someone in danger. They use first aid kits to treat injuries.

rescue board
a board used to help swimmers float

15

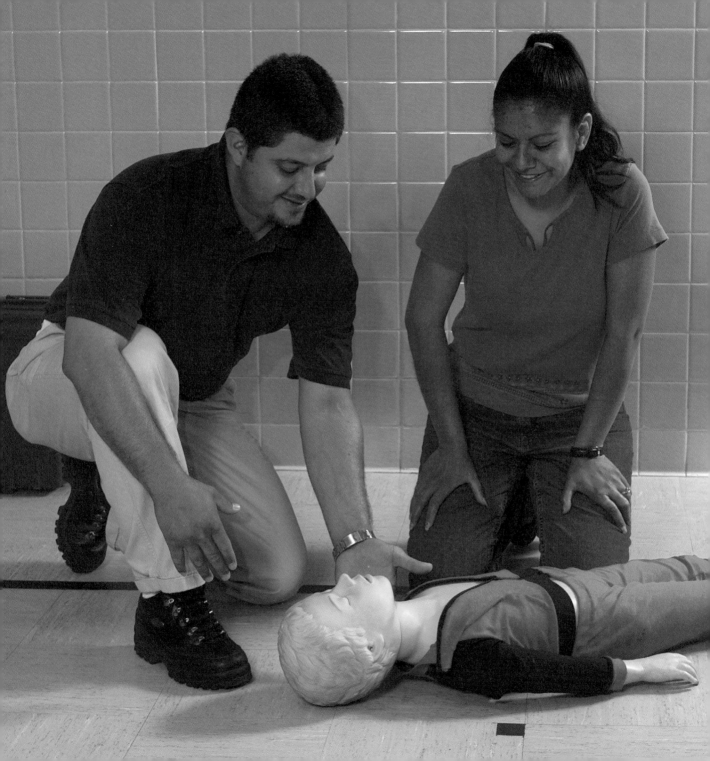

Lifeguards and Training

Lifeguards must take swimming and safety classes. They learn how to carry people to safety. They learn how to use first aid kits to treat injuries. Lifeguards learn CPR. CPR is a way of restarting a heart that has stopped beating. People must pass tests to become lifeguards.

POOL RULES

1. WALK. DON'T RUN.
2. DO NOT DIVE INTO MAIN POOL.
3. NO DUNKING OR HORSEPLAY IN OR AROUND POOL.
4. DO NOT SPLASH OR VISIT WITH LIFEGUARDS.
5. NO SMOKING, EATING, OR CHEWING GUM IN POOL AREA. POP MUST BE KEPT IN TABLE AREA.
6. 3 LOUD BLASTS ON WHISTLE MEANS CLEAR POOL.

LIFEGUARD

People Who Help Lifeguards

Lifeguard instructors teach lifeguards how to keep swimmers safe. They make sure lifeguards can notice injuries and prevent emergencies. Lifeguards work together by taking turns watching people swim. Swimmers help lifeguards by following safety rules.

prevent
to stop something
from happening

How Lifeguards Help Others

Lifeguards keep swimmers safe. They watch swimmers and help them follow safety rules. Lifeguards try to keep emergencies from happening. Lifeguards help people stay safe and have fun in the water.

Hands On: Water Safety Memory Game

Swimmers help lifeguards by following water safety rules. You can make a game to learn water safety rules.

What You Need

Water safety rules from the photograph on page 18
12 index cards
Pencil or pen
Markers or crayons
Friend

What You Do

1. Copy each water safety rule on an index card.
2. Draw a picture of each rule on the other index cards. Draw only one picture on each picture card.
3. Place the cards upside down in rows.
4. Turn over one card, then another card. If the cards match, keep both cards and try to match two more cards.
5. If the cards do not match, it is your friend's turn.
6. Keep playing until all of the cards are matched.

Watch swimmers the next time you are at the pool. See if other people know water safety rules as well as you do. Try to help other swimmers follow the rules.

Words to Know

CPR (SEE PEE AR)—short for cardiopulmonary resuscitation; CPR is a way of restarting a heart that has stopped beating; lifeguards must know how to do CPR.

emergency (e-MUR-juhn-see)—a sudden or dangerous event that must be handled quickly

first aid kit (FURST AYD KIT)—a set of items such as bandages and tape; lifeguards use first aid kits to help people in emergencies.

injury (IN-juh-ree)—damage or harm to the body

prevent (pri-VENT)—to stop something from happening

recreation center (rek-ree-AY-shuhn SEN-tur)—a place where people can swim, exercise, and play sports

warn (WORN)—to tell about a danger that might happen in the future

Read More

Boelts, Maribeth. *A Kid's Guide to Staying Safe around Water.*
The Kid Library of Personal Safety. New York:
PowerKids Press, 1997.

Raatma, Lucia. *Safety at the Swimming Pool.* Safety First!
Mankato, Minn.: Bridgestone Books, 1999.

Internet Sites

Child and Family Canada—Water Safety
http://www.cfc-efc.ca/docs/cccf/00000138.htm
United States Coast Guard—Water 'n Kids
http://www.uscg.mil/hq/g-cp/kids/WaterNKids/cvr.html
United States Lifesaving Association
http://www.usla.org/index.shtml

Index